ANCHOR
BOOKS

*A New Day Has Come*

Edited by

Chiara Cervasio

To Mary

Best Wishes

from Kay

Jude

Sept 2004

X

First published in Great Britain in 2004 by
ANCHOR BOOKS
Remus House,
Coltsfoot Drive,
Peterborough, PE2 9JX
Telephone (01733) 898102

SB ISBN 1 84418 343 2

# FOREWORD

Anchor Books is a small press, established in 1992, with the aim of promoting readable poetry to as wide an audience as possible.

We hope to establish an outlet for writers of poetry who may have struggled to see their work in print.

The poems presented here have been selected from many entries, and as always editing proved to be a difficult task.

I trust this selection will delight and please the authors and all those who enjoy reading poetry.

Chiara Cervasio
Editor

# CONTENTS

## SHREDDERS

They go through the shredder,
Pride, self-respect and innocence,
Leaving you two choices:
1 - crouch among the litter and try
To piece it back together -
Or 2 - pulp it,
Create yourself a fresh sheet of paper
And cut it in two.
On one piece write 'I'm sorry',
And on the other, 'I forgive myself'.

*Pablo Rose*

## CHAPTER AND VERSE

Our lives are like an open book
With a beginning, middle, end
How we fill our pages
Are down to us my friend
No Tippex, no editing
No chance to change the past
Every day a new page filled
The old ones fading fast

As we flick back through our pages
And reflect upon our life
The good, the bad, the ugly
The trouble and the strife
Our memories are now history
No editing in our life

Some like to leave their pages blank
Some like to fill them fast
We can only fill what's present
With some regrets of past
When we have finished here on Earth
Our book is then complete
All earthly pages written
And fired in the heat
We go to meet our maker
Who edits in discreet
All errors wiped away
Our legacy lives on
For loved ones we have left behind
Who carry memories on

*Mark Tann*

# A NEW BEGINNING?

*Happy New Year, Happy New Year,*
So many voices make this loud cheer.
When they wake the following morn
How many resolutions will have been born?
No more chocolate, no more booze
Ensure the wife has five minutes' snooze!
Promises made without a care,
Life is more than chocolate, so beware.

We could all make a more solemn vow
To respect all cultures and religions now.
Have we really learnt from others bad deeds?
Can we remember how to plant good seeds?
All the world's children have fertile brains
An ideal land to grow good grain.
Food to fill cold and empty hearts
Then maybe another war will not start.

If this food is shared amongst us all
Children of the world may grow proud and tall.
Look upon others with a smile and a cheer
No harsh words or blood spilled here!
Remember how many fertile minds
Were wantonly destroyed by a land mine.
Words are worth more than guns and shields
This money could be spent on a farm's bare field.

Happy days and quiet nights,
Each new dawn bringing soft clear light.
Look at the clock, midnight draws near,
Then all join hands and get ready to cheer,
We have kept one resolution, right from the beginning
A happy New Year we have the right to be singing!

***Jean Easson***

## THE BEGINNING (GENISIS CHAPTER 1)

In the beginning God created the heavens
The Earth too in His way
It needed light as well as dark
All this in the very first day

In day two the sky was formed
A huge expanse so vast
Below, the waters of the seas
With rippling waves that dance

The third day God created land
With many plants and trees
'Behold there shall come forth some life
With each, there shall be seeds'

Upon the fourth day God did make
A huge bright sun for light
It shone by day upon the ground
And the moon He made for night

Next came living creatures
On land and sea was life
Birds flew up in the sky
This happened on day five

Day six the animals all were made
All livestock on the ground
Finally in His image
God made man from dust around

'I give you everything upon the Earth
In sky or in the sea
I brought them forth from nothing
To praise and worship me'

God saw all that He'd made
Then on the seventh morn
Took rest from all the work He'd done
The whole Earth now was born!

*Jo Taylor*

## LIFE IS FOR LIVING

I wish it were tomorrow, Mum. Why won't tomorrow come?
That is the day for doing what today just can't be done.

Don't wish you time away Child; life passes soon enough.
The planet's bright and beautiful. Even though life's tough.

I wish it were tomorrow, Mum. For playing with my friends;
an only child's a lonely child. Tomorrow loneness ends.

Don't wish your time away Child; life passes soon enough.
The planet's bright and beautiful. Even though life's tough.

I wish it were tomorrow, Mum. When I'll be leaving school;
there's been no fun, no pleasure. They treat me like a fool.

Don't wish your time away Child; life passes soon enough.
The planet's bright and beautiful. Even when life's rough.

I wish it were tomorrow, Mum. When Dave and I get wed;
I think he really loves me. At least, that's what he's said.

Don't wish your time away Child; life passes soon enough.
The planet's bright and beautiful. Even though life's tough.

I wish it were tomorrow, Mum. My baby being born;
when I'll be slim and trim again. Not fat and all forlorn.

Don't wish your time away Child; life passes soon enough.
The planet's bright and beautiful. Even when life's rough.

I wish it were tomorrow. Young Gracie as a bride;
her father standing next to me. His breast beating with pride.

Oh, Mum. If it were yesterday. With you still by my side?
I'd have the chance to hold you, that sad dark day you died.

I'm scared about tomorrow, Mum. The light is fading fast.
If only it were yesterday - and I could change what's past.

*Anita Richards*

## FIRST JANUARY 2004

What will you bring us, strange new year?
Doubts and troubles, pain and fear?
Or will you at last give heartening sun,
A promise of better days begun?
Hope for less hatred, growing trust
In God and man, as indeed we must
If life can endure, as so close we dwell
And so much is found that could serve as well,
So may we resolve to combat pain,
Our beautiful Earth to restore again,
Our animal friends to make their way
Unmolested, and helped from day to day.
May children daily in safety walk
Not endangered by adults with specious talk.
With time to develop as nature decrees
While honest affection their pathway frees.
Oh God, whose plan we cannot know,
Too vast for our minds which slowly grow,
Make us wiser, not cleverer, so we beseech,
That our place in Your pattern at last we reach.

*Kathleen M Hatton*

# A WANDERING MAN

Now Adam was a wandering man, he travelled far and wide,
And when he left his family, his wife and children cried;
They hung on him and clung on him and begged him not to go,
But Adam set his heart and said: 'I simply must!' and so,

He packed his bags, went on his way without a 'by-your-leave',
And when his years of absence grew his wife and children grieved;
But finally they dried their eyes, with all their passion spent,
When many years passed by with not a card or letter sent.

For Adam had abandoned all to start a brand new life,
And blind ambition left no thought or care for kids or wife.
His luck was in, he prospered well, indulged his every whim,
Great riches, fame, and gorgeous women threw themselves at him.

He'd want for nothing, life was grand, his selfishness had paid,
There was no question in his mind, the right decision made.
But over-excess over time meant Adam's health grew poor,
And as it failed his thoughts returned to family once more.

Mortal thoughts possessed his mind and fears of end of life,
So Adam took a pad and penned a letter to his wife.
He did not know that she had gone, with children now all grown
The time was right for her to start a new life of her own.

The postman brought the letter back and Adam got depressed,
For on the envelope was scrawled: 'Not known at this address'.
Poor Adam wept; with failing heart he knew he'd soon be dead;
'Ah me, poor me, my life will end,' was what our wanderer said,

'With no one here to bury me, in sorrow wail and weep,
To eulogise my memory or sing me to my sleep,
A rich and selfish life I've lived and now I die alone,
It is my fate, I see too late, to reap what I have sown.'

*Janet Greenwood*

## JANUARY

Jaded decorations, billowing in the breeze
Soaked through from December rains,
A deflated Santa - drooping, forlorn
No Christmas cheer remains.
Twinkling lights, that were strategically placed
With such careful consideration,
Hang listlessly now, on an old oak tree -
Their removal a cause of frustration.
For this garden that was bathed in glorious light
Is now stripped of all its glitter;
A wondrous sight to behold no more . . .
. . . January blows in, on a wind that's so bitter.
Darkness descends as a Christmas cracker escapes
It skips in the wind now, it's free
From refuse bags full of discarded remains . . .
. . . A gluttonous pile of debris.
Yet I watch through the window at the slate-grey sky
And my spirit is lifted from gloom;
For lurking around New Year's corner -
Will be spring and its wonderful bloom.

*Jane Nolan*

# AND FINALLY, I'VE MOVED ON

I was having a bad time of it, see, about fifteen months or so back
I didn't think the move was working, perhaps it was time to hit the track
Back to the slums of Hackney, where it's nothing but poverty
                                        and despair
Where violence is a commonplace occurrence, and nobody
                                        seems to care.

Where filthy syringes can be found, laying on the steps of blocks
                                        of flats
And grubby tramps sit deploringly, waiting for money to land in
                                        their hats
Where fear and intimidation rule the streets, anguish upon many a face
A more despicable area of London, I have not been able to trace.

Where walls of giant tower blocks, are daubed with messages of hate
And every day brings despondency, because you don't know your fate
Where people lay ensnared in their isolation, trapped in a prison cell
In their own little world of desolation, imprisoned in their own shell.

Where crimes against the human being, take place every other day
Where children are trapped into this way of life, not allowed out to play
Where bestial monstrosities known as man, seek prey from slitted eyes
Not stopping their horrible perverted actions, when an innocent
                                        youngster dies.

And me, a man of intelligence, wanted to return to all of this?
Not thinking of my current harmony, not reflecting on what I
                                        would miss
No! Before you suggest it, depression hadn't got inside my head
Perhaps I'd just found it so difficult, to sever that final thread.

A thought ran through my mind that day, imagine it if you can,
*You can take the man out of Hackney, but you can't take Hackney*
                                        *out of the man*
The television was on that night, and surprise registered when I heard
A television personality say exactly the same thing, really,
                                        word for word.

Now coincidence is a funny thing, and shock hit me in the mind
Perhaps it was a message telling me, to leave all this serenity behind
If I had been a complete fool, taking it as a message he was trying to tell
I couldn't have fallen any further, than back on the road to a living hell.

Determination is a wonderful thing, it can exist without one
                                        even knowing
Like the planting of a new seed, except inside your mind it's growing
I wouldn't want to return there, placing myself again on a torture rack
And I think I've finally managed to move on, and can never ever
                                        go back.

*B W Ballard*

# I WAIT

Winter's come,
I wait
For the wonderland of
Crisp white snow.

Bitter winds blow
Through my body,
Ice cold rain drenches my soul
No winter wonderland for me.

No snowman, no icicles
Just memories frozen behind
Closed doors.

Waiting, still waiting.

*Carole Taylor*

## JANUARY SONG

Blackbird singing in the skeleton tree
sing your song, bird, just for me.
The sky's a cage that sets you free,
and I'll never be your master.

Mole unseen, with unseeing eyes
in darkness underneath the ice,
beneath my feet your kingdom lies
but I'll never be your master.

Strips of snow folded into the ground,
you fell from the sky without a sound
and when you have gone I'll still be around,
though I'll never be your master.

For a master of nothing am I,
trudging round Oval Park,
beneath a sky so lacking in cheer
while my heart like a flute
pipes its bitter-sweet notes
into January air.

*Peter Bauer*

## SUNRISE

Here all night
in rocking wind we sleep
watched by stars
lulled by seas slumbering deep

listen, in dawn's chill
lark awakened cries
out over the sea
we see sun's ball rise

world is born again
in tide of purple and gold
land's soul is filled
with dreams untold

*T Webster*

## NEW BEGINNING

There is a time in one's life when things must change.
We all have to sort out lives, new visions to arrange.
Time to step forward and follow your dreams.
Walk forward in life, over hills and by streams.

You will pick up the heart that you thought was lost.
For the memories of romance have long since been lost
Collect up the pieces that were once broken and torn.
No longer shall you see your life as forlorn.

The doormat you will no longer offer to be.
For you can be loved for whom you are, wait and see.
You have sat all alone, cried your last tears.
Now is the time to cast off all your fears.

This new beginning you have been looking for
Is just waiting for you to step through your door.
Do not wait for life to come rolling by.
Before that will happen you will surely die.

Grab every chance that comes your way.
Live every moment to the full each day.
Love and romance will come your way.
For this new beginning is here to stay.

*Jo Lodge*

## THE FOUR SIGNS

Often I have thought through long and empty hours
of pains and lessons unconsumed, lost to wayside bowers,
where sense is just a privileged wasteland
its dark cultured fissures deadly to man, there,
flayed ambitions exposed to mirth
cling to a bank where a river once ran.
Darkness closed its corners round me
I thrashed in the agony of a latent man,
of giddying ideas plucked from slumber
some gave light and so I began.
Through eye-dimpled windows, was I meant to see?
Attic salt wigs sparred in tar-clouded parlours
I moved to their ministries, such a lonely affair,
to gulp at their wit, high traces unheard
shackled with the devil on a rack of despair.
Towards me an infinite puzzle of pieces scrambled
to somewhere in my mind, paused to reflect on this
heaviside layer, margins to escape and leave behind;
and so it was, disorder startled by a waking freshness
inward and matchless stiffened in a manner fearless
to none, I gathered my chattels and
forged a raised mark, as never before,
mind and tongue assembled as one.
Eminent counsels had written their worth; devouring onward
such learning transcended all I had known, a broad
path inspired, unfolded before me, its wariness aroused
my choking dullness; forwardly stumbling, intense but lively,
there brushed at the pile, savaged every rule -
was there ever a moment for turning a fool?
An unlettered long sleep brought wildness to kerb
I steadied excess; should illusion glow? Incensed but just, my
error dissolved and I was wedded to eternal day;
the musk of spring held fast my heel.
would blithe spirits soar, had I to re-think,
those barriers intact might they fall to me?

Be hero or rebel, row alone, deepest impulse of theirs
little known, that my new prospect shall struggle more
but things of knowledge entice and please;
as ever, the seemingly masquerade
their tasks unreached, yet entertain,
what irks the slothful keep alive and merry life retain.

***Tom Griffiths***

## 2004

A new year
Full of enthusiasm
Cheerfulness and excitement
What is in store!
Not known but living in hope
A bright star
Is shining in the new heaven
Love is waking in abundance
One must wallow
In the new clean clear waters
That flow in the mind and heart
2004, here we come!

*Alma Montgomery Frank*

## MANY NEW BEGINNINGS

Amy is a lucky girl, her parents' longed-for priceless pearl,
Born profoundly deaf, consultant said,
Undefeated; both quickly learned to sign, instead,
Hour upon hour Amy sat on Mummy's lap
As she taught her to lip-read, worthwhile stop-gap,
Grandparents learned sign language, too,
To help Amy to chat, by hand, in lieu,
She was later given numerous tests
For the hospital to assess
About a cochlea implant;
Gain to nth degree; NHS immovable slant.
At two Amy had delicate five-hour op;
Now five, clearly chatters, happily non-stop,
Eager to learn, teachers fast to discern
No more needs a class side-assistant
In mainstream school, fully co-existent
With hearing children to work and play;
Gratitude be to God and medical world today.

Removes her implement to sleep,
Sudden silence causes her to weep,
Daddy lies on floor holding her hand
Until she slumbers into dreamland.
Nothing and no one halts Daddy's routine
From 'wolf-in-the-wood and big teeth' scene.

Amy has many new beginnings
She's not fazed, bats on in her innings,
This week from nursery to infant school
She's looked forward to all through festive Yule,
New baby brother she shows all with pride,
Teaching and bossing him until he's wide-eyed.
Her folk? Willing to aid, parents whose babe born with hearing unmade.

*Hilary Jill Robson*

## SSH . . . LISTEN

Listen to the birdsong
Listen to the way the wind blows
Listen to the children's laugh
Listen to the way this poem goes
Listen to your mind
Listen to your heart
Listen to the old lady's words so kind
Know, listen
Listen to the shouting
Listen to the children's cry
Listen to the guns
Listen to the mothers screaming, 'Why?'
Listen to the people's words of hate
Listen to the silence when it's over
Listen to your fate

It's a new year, a new start
Let's hold each other up instead of falling apart

*Jeni Letham  (16)*

# In 2004

I'm glad that last year's gone away
And dropped into the past
I'm glad that years do come and go
Never meant to last
For last year was a nightmare
So many broken dreams
But funny every year's the same
Or so it always seems
But I know this year is different
I feel it in the air
Something great will happen
I may find love declared
It may be that I'll write a book
Or paint a huge success
Achievements are within my grasp
I know I'll have no rest
I plan to visit countries
I've never seen before
To feel the wind upon my face
While walking on the shore
I plan to write a novel
Tending it with care
And I plan to paint a picture
That will make each person stand and stare
They seem so huge these tasks of mine
But I plan not to be poor
In my year of fame and fortune
Just labelled two thousand and four

*Patricia H Moore*

## LIFE CAN MOVE ON

Oh how can this be? Why is life doing this to me?
I am ready to move on with this new life that's just begun
Why do I sense that he is not sure?
Despite all that's gone on before
All I want is a bit of joy
From this man I've known from a boy
A bit of love and affection
When I reach out in his direction
The past I have put behind
The sad things unwelcome in my mind
Can he not see that this I can do?
But it is not just me, it is also you
Can you move on and forget some of before?
Can you smile and be happy when you walk through the door?
I have been evolving for some time now
Dealing with your actions, don't always know how
I know I am now ready to do this
Some of the past I certainly won't miss
But some of my thoughts and understandings will be different to yours
A difference of opinions, nothing more
You have caused me much sorrow and pain
But I am willing to trust that you won't do that again
You can't be angry at how I've felt
Be proud of the way that I have dealt
Don't doubt my strength and ability to move on
It's certainly not lost, it's all the more strong
Your decision was made for the right reasons I hope
But were you sure that you'd be able to cope
Don't give up on us now we've fought for so long
Please be happy, please be strong

*Amanda Bailey*

# NEW YEAR'S ASPIRATIONS

In what we do
And where we go
To what we achieve
In our New Year's aspiration

Hold up your head
And let's be counted
For work that's been
Well done

Reach out and help
Promises heartfelt
To all our friends
And neighbours

A brand New Year
For us to cheer
Love, hope and celebration

*Margery Rayson*

## MOVING ON

Got sick of saying yes
When I should be saying no
Got tired of going places
I didn't want to go

I guess the light went out
The candle burned away
No point in trying anymore
No reason for to stay

It's over when it's over
When the spark has gone
No passion left, no laughter
Time for moving on

*John Robinson*

# PORTRAIT OF MAN

With veins that run deep into my soul
Vessels more precious than pure gold
A being so uniquely defined
Beauty that cannot be denied
Full of life
Hope
History
Of goodness
Grace
Destiny
From a perfect model moulded
By mighty, masterful hands
An awesome creature
No small wonder
I am a man

*John D Evans*

# LANDING IN THE THIRD AGE

Grey power
Grey hair
One leaves chance to advance
The other not fair

Pension income
Budget rake
One leaves doors closing
The other an ache

Routine gone
Adaptation
One leaves a rupture
The other indigestion

Funny thing
Thinking time
One leaves a question
The other portal sublime

Old age
Senior citizen
One leaves distaste
The other a partisan

Fair dues
Human rights
One leaves something lacking
The other hope in lights

So be it
Time to kill
One leaves resigned acceptance
The other space to fill

Grey power
Grey hair
One leaves scope for contribution
The other says beware!

*P A Findlay*

## THOUGHTS OF A BETTER WORLD

Christmas last year wasn't mere cheer
those lost family from afar suddenly felt quite near
life had new meaning like the Bethle'm star.

Family and friends *truly* felt so dear
front door always ajar, no envies or enemies to fear
food *was* fit for kings from every bazaar.

*Can it all last?* I think out loud and clear
no evil deed should mar, peace *should* last all year
America, Egypt, China and darkest Africa.

Then His will fulfilled, nations *shall* steer
clear of war, hatred's scar, onward thro' this new year
and grow together, a world on even par.

Divine revelation ignored, unheeded, *is* here
worldly beings receive secret formula *all* year, each year
God and man to act out Heaven's spectacular.

***Christopher Barnes***

## FRIENDS

Should old acquaintance be forgot
Now the brand new year is here?
Should we not give a single jot
Or should we hold them very dear?

As years go by they've stuck like glue,
Through thick and thin they're there,
Years come and go from old to new,
Without friends 'twould be hard to bear.

Some come and go just like the sun,
They warm you for a while,
They entertain you; they're such fun,
With their oh such sunny smile.

But best friends are there through thick and thin,
They share the good and bad,
They do not leave you on a whim,
To have them you're so glad.

So at the changing of the year,
We raise a glass or two,
                    To all our friends both far and near,
Without them what would we do?

With friends we don't just pass the time,
We visit, phone and write,
And as we sing of Auld Lang Syne,
We think of them tonight.

*Margaret Blight*

## NEW YEAR

Old year now ends,
Greetings ascend,
New year song sends,
Happy New Year.

Fireworks give vent,
Colours are rent,
The firmament
Painted and clear.

Streamers fall down,
Balloons are blown,
No one alone,
Crowds holding hands.

Champagne explodes,
Old year now folds,
In each abides
Hopes for our lands.

Promises are made,
Broken then fade,
Water cascade,
Fountains will sing.

Cold the year starts,
Wait for the art,
Nature's leaves part,
Enter fresh spring.

*David M Walford*

# A New Year Is Given

They say a new year has begun.
The dreams, the wishes, and the joys.
Peace and good will.
Hope and love given all around.

What if it is not a new year?
Could it be the same one,
Like the one so long ago,
That started with a gift?

The god that gave a gift,
A son, a man for everyone?
What are we supposed to see
In this gift that was given?

Was he the one to show
The world how to share?
But what was done,
What was taken?

A man, a thought, a gift,
That no one shall go hungry
Or thirsty;
This world was given as a gift.

They say a new year has begun,
Let's hope that all are treated fairly.
No more hunger, no more despair,
Let's hope this gift we all will share.

*R Mills*

# A BETTER WORLD

This busy lifestyle of today, no time to kill, no standing still,
Progression to - we know not where,
Time now to pause, to be aware
Of change, be it bad or good,
That will affect our livelihood.

Birth control to be observed, pregnant mums with empty tums,
Food for third world's populations,
Drugs to help fight dire infections,
Take heed for when the die is cast,
All will know its grim repast.

Man's greed for money, deforestation, destroying God's creation,
Dumb animals and tribal man
From axe and chainsaw quickly ran.
Centuries of peaceful life
Gone, with bloodshed, pain and strife.

Horizons blocked by concrete jungles, destroying health,
Pursuit of wealth,
Stress, a killer, all-consuming
As on the dark horizon looming,
Global warming, poisonous gasses -
Devastation of the masses.

Take action now, to stem the tide, reform, set ill aside,
Let nature's power change ill to good,
Restore man's pride, his livelihood,
No more hunger, free from pain,
Till the soil, sow the grain.

Working together, restore tomorrow's world, with flag unfurled,
March forward with determination,
Achieve - improve - help every nation,
Banish gasses, pollution, grime,
It can be done - *it just needs time.*

***Pamela Carder***

# RESOLUTION

Tears have made my pillow soggy
Someone hurt me, called me podgy
Been eating food that's far too stodgy
*I'm going on a diet*

That comment left me broken-hearted
Got me thinking, got me started
Me and fat will soon be parted
*Now I'm on a diet*

Chips and chocolate have been banished
Till this podginess has vanished
Even though I'm feeling famished
*I'm sticking to my diet*

Whatever I wear I'm looking frumpy
Can't bear feeling fat and lumpy
If others think of me as dumpy
*Nothing will break my diet*

This is my pledge and solemn vow
That starting here and starting now
I'll lose this weight someway, somehow
*I'm committed to this diet*

**S Brewer**

## NEW YEAR

This is the time to make a fresh start
for a new year has just begun,
plan for the future and live for today
as the past has already been done.

It's time for people to make resolutions
of the things they want to achieve,
bring forward the good times
and hope for some more,
but the bad times I think we should leave.

So here's to a new year
let peace be with you,
and good luck for the future
in all that you do.

*Rachael Ford*

## NEW YEAR'S EVE

A day is dying,
twilight is fading;
night is crying,
breaking dawn
dribbling,
as joyful tears
of a new hope
fall softly
like morning dews
of a new year,
washing away
dusts of a dreary
season.

***Senator Ihenyen***

## NEW YEAR'S REVOLUTION

Not going to promise new habits this year
nor think up some weird resolutions.
Refusing to change the old patterns, my dear,
or any new quick-fix solutions.

I won't give up smoking or turn down that drink
to stop me from feeling unhealthy.
Won't go to the gym or buy trainers and thongs.
The cost only leaves me un-wealthy.

That filing will stay in the pile as it was,
I know just where everything's dumped.
Any misguided attempts to help 'sort'
will end up with somebody thumped.

The scales will stay gathering dust on the floor,
I won't even notice they're there.
The magazine hints about fighting the bulge
will not see my diet laid bare.

I'll think about diets for holidays when
I need to squeeze in my bikini.
'Til then I'll continue to pamper myself
with cigarettes and a Martini.

***Ali Paterson***

# In The Outer Limits Of Nowhere

On a dry barren landscape live the forgotten people,
Scantily clad figures of a hunger-stricken civilisation.
Shadows of sorrow towering over lost, mystified souls,
Ribcages fastened together with strings of living tissue,
Covering only a vacuum of emptiness, waiting, waiting -
Searching for the means to why and how.
The answers are not easily supplied,
As continuing pity and hardship stride in everlasting dominance.
Teeth so brittle grind a breadcrumb to dust,
Gripping a slender hope of faith and belief,
Each single drop of grateful moisture,
Swallows hurt, pride and purpose,
Gulped so hard with utmost expectations,
Brings with it - a new beginning.
A colourful dawn of anticipation rises,
Each ray of light holds promise and deliverance,
From the cruel cycle of critical circumstance.
Endurance weeps with joys of survival,
As yet another day slowly disappears in the sunset.
Mother famine gives birth in blind ignorance,
Overpopulated children of starvation choke and suffocate,
Unloved and deserted, troubled and weary,
As a production line produces more with so little to offer,
This can only cancel out too many tomorrows,
For those to whom I have already -
Said my last goodbye.

*Nigel Astell*

# PHASES

My world is all crazy
And I'm going insane
For everything changes
As you lose what you gain

The weight that I carry
Burdens my mind
For the shadows I'm chasing
Have crept up behind

My heart was once lightness
Now it's the darkest of hue
For the phases are changing
And I'm changing too

The dreams I have witnessed
Have crumbled to dust
And the memories of laughter
Have a double-edged thrust

My world is all crazy
Oh what can I do
As everything changes
And I'm beginning anew

It's confusing; oh so confusing

*I Graham*

# NOT ABOUT WMD (WEAPONS OF MASS DESTRUCTION)

The war in Iraq of 2003 was not about weapons of mass destruction
The war in Iraq was based on the colour of oil
The war in Iraq was illegal with no support
George Bush lied to the American people about the illegal war in Iraq
His main purpose was to get re-elected in 2004 as president of the USA
It was not about weapons of mass destruction
It was not about weapons of mass destruction
The war in Iraq was based on oil
It was not about democracy and freedom
They called it liberation and freedom
I called it occupation, I called it occupation and it is not freedom and
                                                    it is oppression
It was not about weapons of mass destruction
It was not about weapons of mass destruction
The occupation of Iraq was based on oil
The occupation of Iraq was based on human rights violations by
                                    American and British troops
Tony Blair lied to the British people about the illegal war in Iraq
His main purpose was to get the oil supplies from the occupation of Iraq
It was not about freedom and democracy in Iraq
It was not about weapons of mass destruction
It was not about weapons of mass destruction.

*Errol Baptiste*

## GIVE US MORE

In case of love
There is not enough of it.

The government
Cuts the services
To those in dire need.

In case of dire need
Those in it
Are the most damaged
The most rejected
Those acquainted with loss.

In case of loss
We all know it
Experience grief
Accept bereavement
As part of life.

In case of life
It is to be lived
Not cocooned or settled
Experience the unexpected
Living free.

In case of freedom
We need to know it.
Given a stake
In a free society
Knowing love.

In case of love,
There is never enough of it.

*Irene Clare Garner*

# A WALK IN THE PARK

The sun penetrates the room with beautiful new rays,
and my eyes awaken on a brand new day.
The baby fledglings are singing with an early morning song,
and I've been granted another day with breath in my lungs.
The streets are busy with the rush of people with an aim,
to achieve and accomplish is the name of the game.
As I stroll along and head through the park,
I capture many snapshots before it gets dark.
The butterflies hover lightly around in the sky,
with a vivid memory of the day they learnt how to fly.
The petals open on flowers so bright,
and the leaves on the trees, what a fabulous sight.
The distinctive smell of blades of new grass,
which we inhale until the warm smell has passed.
The rush of fresh water ejects from a spring,
a refreshing feeling when you take that first drink.
When one is blessed with a glorious sunny day,
it brings back cherished memories of brides on their way.
The big day arrives and the wedding cars are due,
and the moment arrives when you both say I do.
New couple's love binding and setting up home,
and preparing for a future with new seeds being sown.
New babies being born and letting out that first cry,
and parents proudly announce, 'The new child is mine.'
And one can't forget the anxiety within,
when you start a new job and you're travelling in.
The clock strikes five and you're oh so glad,
on reflection your first day at work wasn't bad.
A new moon appears and darkens the sky,
as I drift off to sleep and dream on a high.
My heart will be joyous and will always be singing,
as long as each day we can share new beginnings.

***Steven Howe***

## NEW BEGINNINGS

Bright and wonderful, new beginnings,
Where cherished dreams dance merrily,
With great expectations, with hope to come,
Whilst focusing, whilst brain-searching,

With commitment, planting dreams thoroughly,
Loyally and devoted, whilst dedicated to achieve
The impossible dream, new beginnings bring blessings,
Fundamentally yours by right,

Whilst conquering all dark phantoms,
On the steadfast path of light,
Staying focused, whilst flying with angels,
With determination's quest, and resilience strong,

With faith's guiding banner,
Conquering all possibilities,
Like a champion of the night,
Whose demons come to fright,

With absolute authority, and love,
With better conditions for all peoples of the world,
Where democracies' chains unfold,
Giving everyone an equal chance,

To love and learn, to succeed,
Bringing unity and understanding,
In a competitive world turning,
With unlimited opportunities for all the citizens of the world,

Where numerous children die alone,
Not knowing of brotherly and sisterly love,
Where loving people ask why
Where God works mysteriously above,

Not giving us all the answers we seek,
So humankind can learn with selfless labour and love.

*James S Cameron*

## LOVE AT FIRST SIGHT

One glance in your direction and I was smitten from the start
Love was like an arrow piercing my heart
The first time that I saw your face
My pulse took on a faster pace
The first time that I held you, I loved you from the start
I can't believe the love I feel
It can't be true, it seems unreal
Tears of happiness and joy
What a gorgeous baby boy
A gift from Heaven up above
Sent for his grandma to give him love

*D E Henry*

## NEW BEGINNING

It was one year ago when I nearly died from a 'bleed' in the brain and my family cried.
I had no idea I'd been taken so ill and how I recovered, put down to God's will.

The doctors and nurses I always admired for how they looked after me and never tired.
Of making quite sure that they all did their best to see to my comfort, gave plenty of rest.

For days I just hovered, it was touch and go, prayers were then offered, my friends told me so.
But now I am better and well on my way, to a new beginning I have to say.

Thank you, Lord, for your mercy and grace, I look forward to spring with a smile on my face.

*Patricia Pratt*

## PROSAIC THANKS TO MY REMOTE LANDLORD

Dear Mr Taylor

From Zimbabwe I came back to start;
Each die rolled; I scored a double six,
Advancing to the pinnacle of good fortune.

Your flat and Wadebridge's friendly bosom
Have granted me that unespoused belief:
Heaven, but pre- not post-mortem.

Sheer homely luxury,
Cosy, warm spaciousness
And town-centred convenience
For one happily on Shank's pony.

Imbued with an ambience all its own:
A happy flat, as said Mrs Mabley truly.
It lends itself to simple, uncluttered decoration,
With its generous cupboards;
Imparts its vibes
To all my family and new-found friends
And warm-hearted, helpful
Landing neighbouress and neighbourling,
With such expansive, smiling lady agents.

Should you ever come this way
I would be honoured to receive you.

Sincerely

*Eileen Ellis-Whitfield*

## UNSEASONABLE

Unseasonably warm,
Perfect January day,
After last night's terrific rainstorm.

In the blue skies, aircraft vapour tails
Spark the imagination,
Off to the world's sunny parts.

Bees take advantage of an unseasonable fine,
Come out to clear their guts
On someone's washing on a clothes line

On clean sheets,
Unexplained dirty marks,
Means wash again the sheets.

Forecasters forecast big freeze, extreme cold.
Cow parsley, fresh, tender, green.
Sign of rejuvenation be put on hold.

*George B Clarke*

# I Could Take No More

Lots of love and deep affection
I could not find self-protection
Physically and mentally I was abused
Leaving me with a mind confused
Minute by minute week by week
No protection did I seek
Is this what you meant
When you said I would not win it?
It was just playing, there was nothing in it
Night after night
I would lose the fight
Day after day
I took whatever came my way
Stripped of confidence, battered and bruised
Battle after battle that I would lose
Shouting, screaming even yelling
Then came the next day
All the bruises and swelling
This way of torture I kept inside
A smile on my face was there to hide
I did not know which way to turn
When will you ever learn
I had so much hurt and pain inside
So many bitter tears I cried
Then I knew I could take no more
A chapter ended by the closing of the door
A way of life it was to me
Until that day I was set free.

*C Latimer*

## RING OF BEGINNERS 2003

Ring of beginners,
Nerve ends twitching;
Fingers itching
To fish for thoughts
Caught in the water
Of the Test.

Brain cells grinding,
Some finding
They are hooked
In the throes of
Shoals of words;
Fighting to pull them out,
Not let them slip
Untried, to
Race away on the tide.

Ring of beginners,
Taking turns to
Dip a toe into the
Shock of speaking out
Our words, or
Diving deeply to
Surface with our
Naked thoughts;
And burn.

*Janet Bamber*

## NEW YEAR

As new year approaches
We gather our thoughts
Adding the pluses
And deleting the noughts
We all get to making
Resolutions and plans
The year ahead is now
Really all in our hands!
Old friendships rediscovered
Those friends we've left behind
Are just as important
As the new ones that we find!
So as you make your promises
In the post-Christmas quiet
Please try harder with your friends
Than you do with your diet!

*Rowena*

## CHOOSE YOUR OWN ADVENTURE

If only life was as simple as a 'choose your own adventure'
But I will over complicate till I am wearing dentures
Oh if only I remembered those childhood books of awe
Life's trouble and strife could all be sorted;
By simply turning to page forty four!
My mind never again divided
The day's journeys no more a chore!
So this is my new year's resolution
To throw some 'choose your own adventure' into life's mix
Before it becomes a bore.

*Damian Davies*

# HAPPY NEW YEAR

Those who indoctrinate, brainwash, supply.
Why are they not so ready to die?
What awaits the brave Shahid
Is the same that meets the fallen Yid.
So when Arafat walks along the shore
You can bet his belt is not C4
Any belief condoning such murder
Must look again deeper and further
The only way forward regime or nation
Is understanding, negotiation.
We've all made mistakes, all need to learn
Before the 'martyrs' wastefully burn
I don't deny it, it's no great mystery
We've all done much wrong in our history, but
To teach children to hate is wronger than wrong!
Side by side, forward, on.

*Dennis Campion*

## AMBITION

Sliding down mountains of destiny
Eager for opportunity and success
Skipping all the stones of reason
Never knowing what it's like to rest.

Climbing ladders of fortune swiftly
Dreaming of black leather and lace
Living only for complete triumph
No matter what I have to do or face?

Nine to five just won't do
Successful I'll be no matter what?
No matter whose toes I tread on
Ambition is all I've ever sought.

There'll be water in my garden
A pool filled with everything I need
I'll climb the ladder of victory,
All the while watching others in greed.

Along the gold-dust road I'll drive
On the road to success in my fancy car
The stairway to Heaven draws near
The road to success is not very far!

A parking space just for me
Good morning sir I'll hear them say!
You can't say I'm not ambitious
When I say goodbye to yesterday!

An office as big as a house
On the best of leather I'll sprawl
Life will never be wanting
My ambition is to be best of all!

*Rose Murdoch*

## NEW YEAR 2004

To start a new year, to start a new day
Whatever the consequences, come what may
Not forgetting the misfortunes of the old years
And determined to rectify, any misgiving, without fears.

Thinking ahead of folk, determined to try,
With every effort, want to reach the sky,
Others are happy, to carry on as before
Life is right for them, whatever in store

Planning and dreaming of so many things
To hope and encourage, what the future brings
Determined to achieve some status in life
And remembered in after years, when nostalgia is rife.

So welcome the new year, give it all you can
To build a new future, for one and every man
Wishing for good health, and happiness, now and always
And the joy of good living, for many fine days.

*C King*

# CONSTANTS BURNING!

A hope of yearning
Of emotions returning
Of desires - disconcerting
All consuming - interning
Filling awakening hours
Of needs - constants burning.

*Gary J Finlay*

# A RAY OF FRIENDSHIP

A friendship ray was given,
As a gift to a lonely heart
A bond of pure innocence
A hope of a brand new start . . .

Once a girl so lonesome
As a leaf to a baron tree
To a soul of questions once unknown
Friendship was the key

As the sun beamed down
Upon the team of honesty and trust
The steeple rose through luscious green
A photographic scene
Of must.

Pinching at its sky of blue
Its crew of companionship
A dazzling view

Proud of what was seen before him
A gift of innocence
A friendship given.

*Jodi Wheeler*

# AN INVISIBLE ENTITY

I'm searching for a peaceful land,
A place where tranquillity breeds,
Where I'll find contentment oh so grand -
That will finally meet my needs.
Nowhere on Earth can this place be found,
For it has no sky - it has no ground,
No physical journey can lead me to make the great find,
For I can only arrive there by achieving peace of mind.
Once reached this new entity is mine to keep,
It will heal even the hurt that cuts painfully deep,
I'll feel calmness and peace and serenity galore,
And evil tasks of cruelty shall hurt me no more,
My heart will achieve a state of gladness,
And I'll finally be rid of my painful sadness,
Once I've let my imagination go I can dream anything -
I'll have the freedom to do whatever I choose -
Always to win - never to lose!

*Louise Pamela Webster*

## NEW BEGINNINGS

A new year has begun at dawn
Reflecting on time pass bygone
Reflecting on our past mistakes
Rendering ourselves to get a break

We ask ourselves many questions
Unnerving when we get the answers
What changes are we prepared to make
Or another year of chances to take?

Looking from within
We mirror an image beckoning
Pleading to put our trust
Rather than ending our life in disgust

Please take this newness
And exercise your right
To live your life in defiance
Rather than a plight
Turn a new leaf, start over again
Thanking the image for being your friend
Making it pleasing right through to the end.

*Angela (Nevo) Hopkins*

## THE BABY

This soul, issue of a thousand genesis, as yet unspeech'd
Minimal of comprehension, perpetuate of species which
Raped the earth and lassoed the moon for curiosity,
Whose dextrous digits and computer brains quest universal domination.
See those hands like small starfish sweetly spread
Curling pink tips in reflex movements and lazily flexing thumbs.
What future potentials will they impulse, what traumas see
From those as yet unfocused eyes, still blue with babyness.
What million breaths will fill those lungs, what million heartbeats
Pulse in crawling, toddling, walking, running, racing life?
Who can guess what numbered folk will love this child
Or nascent souls give breath and birthing for tomorrows.
There lies this youngling lulled in milky-bubbled sleep
Carrying the capacity to travel a lifetime unremarked
Or potently to influence the course of posterity.

*Sarah Blackmore*

## FAITH IN LIFE

Let go your soul to the liberty of God's life
offer up your heart and give the Lord,
your faith in life.

Give those around you a loving word
so they may also have faith in life.

Give tenderness to the sick and infirm
so they may also have faith in life.

Give to your enemy give prayer not harm
so they may also have faith in life.

In yourself walk with this vision
so that you will always have faith in life.

To your children teach them compassion
so that they will have faith in life.

*John Clark*

# THE DIET POEM

I've just looked in the mirror
Gosh - who the heck was that
I know I've overdone it
But boy oh boy - that's fat . . . !
Time I think to make a start
First I'll trim my hair
Then I'll shave my legs a bit
But that fat person is still there!
Pluck my eyebrows - trim my nails
Then my teeth I'll floss
I'm standing on the scales now
But not a pound I've lost!
There's only one thing for me to do
Get a grip now if you can
Clean the fridge out double quick
Now this is my 'new plan'!
Chuck out all the chocolate
The cream and all the dips
And all the things you like a lot
That puts fat upon your hips!
Get a tub of Slimfast
Join Weight Watchers with a friend
Put on the 'keep fit' video
And start to puff and bend!
Jog around the block a bit
Join the local gym
Weld yourself in your costume
And go for a nice swim!

Start to eat more healthily
Eat veg and fruit each day
If this fails you can always
Take up religion - and just pray!
That one day you will wake up
And be a perfect '10'
But until that really happens
Cancel all Christmases 'til then!

***Anne E Roberts***

## DUE FOR RENEWAL

Age encroaches, cloud-cocooned, a threat;
living, like old amber, glints.
Shall I savour sunset idylls yet
though my youth has left long since?
A pilgrimage pauses at the base
of still undiscovered peaks,
beauty beckons though a dwindling pace
now impedes my will as speaks,
quietly, voice that only I may hear,
all about the great unknown,
waiting to receive me, drawing near;
close to end I crouch alone;
but rosy mounts are milked with mists,
I cling to the plain, beseech
I be spared where my home exists,
fresh epoch just out of reach.
A year, bitter-sweet, shuts like a gate,
swing-doors encircle my brain;
warming to change I patiently wait,
purpose on earth to attain.
In wearisome channels sleeps remorse;
decrepitude I defy;
unflinching, expectant at the source
of days dreamed of ere I die.

*Ruth Daviat*

## SWEET SIREN SONG

She started
The new year
In the position
And
Juxtaposition
Of one;
Alone and in
Loneness.
So . . .
She sang
Songs of love
Which were
Rumoured to
Have enamoured
Lovers on a
New year
Decades ago.
She sang
As a
Despised
Demimonde.
Each haunting
Note
Became the
Panacea
For her
Loneliness;
Her heart
Besotted
By the
Sweet
Siren song
Of her soul.

*Alice Parris*

## DECEMBER THE THIRTY-FIRST

If you are a party animal,
prone to boozing, probably,
you could whip up some
enthusiasm for the traditional
New Year's Eve ballyhooed bachannal.
I have always felt this
ritual a rather forced euphoria.
As a young man, taking
part in these drunken
revels always left me with
a hollow feeling and an
embarrassed sense of falseness.
It is nice to start
the new year with
a clean slate. But, is
it really so clean?
I mean, how can a dissolute
celebration prepare you for
a new beginning? Oh well,
commit your outrageous
acts on New Year's Eve
and hope your close
relationships survive the trauma.
Go my children, have
a Happy New Year!

*Robert Papcsy*

## NEW BEGINNING

Sparkles in the sunlight
Beckoning us to the view
Once again born, once more anew
Drift to the past only accepts the scorn
Longing, longing for hope to be reborn
A new beginning for us all
A new beginning is our call
Heed these cries, hear this plea
Bring new life, single hope inside me
Silver streams the moonlight
Lights up each soul like a ghost
Dreams of evil lead us astray
And for past sins the souls pay
And what is needed, is hope
And what is heeded, gallow's rope
Crimes we pay for
Settling the score
A new beginning is our plea
A new beginning grows inside me.

*Teresa Whaley*

# RESOLUTIONS

New year resolutions
often sound good at the time
but I find I have a problem
when it comes to keeping mine

*So*

I won't go on a diet
or promise I won't eat
bags of crisps and chocolate
I often buy just as a treat

I won't try to give up smoking
or even to cut down
I'll try not to stop myself
from buying cigarettes in town

And as for drinking alcohol
I will not try to stop
I won't think of moderation
when buying from the shop

I won't be kind and thoughtful
to others who're in need
and when I am out driving
I won't promise I'll not speed

I won't promise to save money
or put any to one side
and I won't cut down on spending
or think - before decide

Maybe if I promise
not to do all kinds of things
then if I break a promise
success is what it brings.

**J L Preston**

## RESOLUTION

The sun sets on another day, the fire burns out again,
The summer's gone, the storm has come,
Feels like the world is at an end,
Thoughts cloud up your mind with doubt
To make hope seem like one in ten,
Well there are brighter skies around the corner,
Here's my advice to you my friend.

Take away your yesterdays and throw them to the wind,
Rip up all those memories and throw them in the bin,
All the dreams that never were to be,
Throw away the tears and sorrow,
Cos tonight we're gonna celebrate,
So let's do it like there's no tomorrow.

When the winds of change blow in your face,
And you cannot understand,
And your faith is questioned once again,
Why things never go as planned,
And the greater picture ever murky paints you feeling down,
Just get back up and start again,
Cos good times they are coming round.

So if the world has let you down again,
Well you're not the only one,
You've just got to see the funny side,
Whenever things go wrong,
For absent friends and family, to all who get along,
Laugh in the face of misery,
And heed the message that's in this song.

*Paul Andrews*

## NEW YEAR'S DAY

Another beginning, another new year,
Another new start is suddenly here,
What will it bring? What will it hold?
Death and disaster? Or joys untold?
We have to wait to see it unfold.
Who knows what will happen,
In this coming year?
When I think of disasters,
I tremble with fear.
Who knows what this new year will bring?
At least we can look forward to spring.
Who knows what will follow after?
Let's hope, we can cope, with smiles and laughter.
So, as we stand on the threshold
Of this new year's day,
Let us hope that good luck
Will come our way.

*Rosanna J Freeman*

# A DECLINE IN CRIME!

I think it is high time there was a decline in crime
How is it these young criminals come to be
As they leave their education and schools behind
Is a mystery to me
I find this so difficult to comprehend
Why should angelic schoolboys suddenly become hell-bent
On theft, arson, robbery and lies, loss of character
In favour of the delinquent mind?
After all to their parents this is so very unkind
Simply to blow their caring minds
And decline into a life of crime
I think it is high time, it's a mystery to me.

*Margaret Bennett*

# WHY AND WHEN AND HOW

What is it that stirs within me now,
A quality of life I have not felt before.
The sun shines brighter,
The sky is lighter,
I am in love
With life.

No longer do I think bad thoughts
Of people
And of things that people do.
For I have learned to cast them out.
To fill my mind with channels new.
I have discovered on looking round
The best things in life
Are easily found.

To look at a primrose in early spring
Is a joy beyond compare.
And the love I see in my granddaughter's eyes
'Neath that crown of jet black hair,
Will make my day quite new again
And clear my mind of mundane things.

Many years it has taken me to acquire this state
The bad times there were many
The good times came late.

For I have reached the stately age
Of three score years and ten,
The age when things don't hurt so much
And I can say where and when.

May I never lose the sense of peace
That lives within me now,
For I have waited a long long time
To know why, and when, and how.

*Vera Jones*

## NOTHING CHANGES

Every single minute a baby is born
New life entering the world
Full of hope and promise
For the future

In the same minute, someone dies
Old life leaving the world
Moving on to another place
Eternal peace and rest

People live their different lives
Learning from the mistakes of the past
Or not, according to their choice
Staying in one place or moving forward

Sometimes going backwards
Re-living outworn behaviour
Painfully aware or unaware
Of those wasted years

Eyes remain closed, ears stopped
Not wishing to face reality
A truth that is so clear
Slamming shut the door of opportunity

So the yearly cycle continues
A repeated pattern revolving
Time comes, time goes
Nothing changes.

*Barbara Manning*

## SEEDS

The flowers you gave me have withered and died
Just like the love you put inside.
You said you would love me through all of time
I never knew love could be so blind.
The scent of the flowers as they died away
Left you dead in my heart today.
Now all I have left are the seeds that fell
For a new special love in my heart to dwell.

*S Bannister*

# PASS ROUND THE WASSAIL BOWL!

The last morsel leaves an empty plate,
The last dreg leaves an empty barrel,
But, the old year leaves an expectant earth -
A new year is born.

The plate is full,
The barrel is overflowing.
Let in the new year -
The Reaper has gone!
Welcome the 'first-footer',
Remember absent friends,
Pass round the Wassail bowl,
A toast -

'To the new year, as yet unknown,
Peace, prosperity, goodwill
And benevolence to all!'

*Joan Thompson*

## BREAK AWAY

Don't do it, don't do it
You will find to your cost
Leaving your home you will be totally lost

Don't do it, don't do it whatever you do
Give up your job with those elderly two
Work in an emporium is so hard to find
For someone who is 50
You're really quite blind

Don't do it, don't do it
Stay safe at home
Remember, oh remember you're not young anymore
I did it, I did it.

*Susan Lewis*

## MY FUTURE

This year to me, has not been too bad,
I've started a career, and a new life too,
My past behind me as been quite sad,
But my future's brighter, with a career to do.

I look to the future,
With hope in my heart,
And a happy view of life,
A positive start.

I'm going to try,
With much strength inside,
To achieve my goal,
To you I confide.

It's going to take time,
And a lot of work too,
To win and succeed,
In the work that I do.

I'll keep on going,
Determined I am,
To create a good future,
And to show the world,
Who I am.

*S Longford*

## JANUARY 1ST

January 1st, new beginning,
What does that mean?
New beginnings on that day,
Are they often seen?

Sometimes,
Maybe sometimes then, new beginnings flow.
But not always, not always,
Isn't that so?

Why celebrate the going?
Who cares to celebrate the leaving of 2003,
With the coming of a new year?
January 1st is just another day to me.

On January 1st,
New beginnings don't just fall at your feet, *kerplunk!*
Raising to golden glory all that has sunk.
Mostly they amble towards you,
Permeate your life, trickling slowly into your veins.
January 1st won't necessarily promise to erase old pressing pains.

Sometimes,
Maybe sometimes then, new beginnings flow.
But not always, not always,
Isn't that so?

January 1st is just another day,
As new ventures travel your way.
January 1st won't necessarily change anything you do or say,
New beginnings arrive on any calendar day.

New beginnings can be dreams come true,
But new beginnings can be a hell too.
The 31st December is given pride of place,
To merrily drink, the old away, but why?

January 1st won't necessarily change,
The tears you cry,
The utterance of sad sighs,
Just by singing 2003 goodbye.

Sometimes,
Maybe sometimes then, new beginnings flow.
But not always, not always,
Isn't that so?

Stepping into January 1st,
Won't necessarily change a thing that day.
We have to change ourselves,
But a *Happy New Year* to the world anyway.

I wish you a *Happy New Year*, 2004,
As the door to 2003 does slam!
With cheers and wishing you good health,
Sincerely from me Carol Ann.

***Carol Ann Darling***

## NEW YEAR'S DAY

Single existence stiff as a board
Anxious to please the public
Good to hear your sweet voice
New Year's Day all over the world

On the floor bare chest
Look up new friends
Make amends for their mistakes
New Year's Day a celebration

Try to make it work
Joke on you
Growing up a pleasure
New Year's Day just the job with pay.

*S M Thompson*

## THE NEW YEAR

So now to review
Good things renew
But bad ones of old
Leave out in the cold
    Nor give them a chance
    With a passing glance.

Keep the path ahead
Clear where feet have led
Life's problems arise
Surmount for the prize
    Worthwhile the effort
    Sort out and abort

So let us pursue
The thoughts ever true
Then happy the days
Improving our ways
    With hope and pleasure
    Gaining such treasure.

***Reg James***

## SOLO

Been dreading this day arriving for a while,
New job pending, said I knew how to file.
But I thought how difficult can it be,
Idiot can do it, maybe old me.

Wondering if I'll like my new workmates,
Must set alarm, I start at half past eight.
If you don't like me the day will drag by,
I'll be emotional, hope I don't cry.

For this will be exciting beginning,
To show everyone, solo, I'm winning.
I have turned my back on last year's lost love,
From adversity, I can rise above.

Although chance to prove just what I can do,
Look forward with much trepidation too.
Because back at work after all those years,
Be natural for me to have some fears.

*S Mullinger*

## PRESENCE

Did something on Mars know of the approach
of not one but two attempts to encroach
on whatever makes up Martian surface
to satisfy a curious Earth race?

Gadget One a cavity can swallow.
From Gadget Two let some pictures follow.
Of a kind not to offer men much scope.
To keep them off Mars, its most fervent hope.

Not entities it intends to invite.
Too greedy, exploitive . . . keen to fight . . .
How strange that while Earthlings probe Martian rock
down on Earth they cannot prevent the shock
of quakes that destroy their houses and lives . . .
yet . . . see how their second Gadget contrives
to send coloured image of rock and stone,
monotony - to make anyone groan . . .
So long as quarrelsome men understand
they need not come here in person to land -

Naturally, a few may make a fuss
about a possible living virus
or some ancient bacteria noted
that in thin air or water once floated.

Here and there, cosmic debris may be thrown
and over all reddish dust may be blown
but - what is packed at either pole not clear
or deeply underlying Gadgets near . . .

For now, in a red - yet reticent mood
a Martian presence continues to brood,
with thought processes we cannot hear,
whose shadow on Earth-screens, does not appear.

*Chris Creedon*

# PROMISES

We've taken down the Christmas cards, and packed away the tree,
Everywhere is looking bare now, surely you must agree,
As we start a 'new year' resolutions once more are made,
Along with the usual 'happy' greetings, that everyone is bade,
Stop smoking, go on that diet, and try harder to keep fit,
The usual list we always make, nothing new, you must admit
Do we wish for 'peace on Earth' and pray it's trouble free,
With no more wars or violent crime, and no poverty?
In our troubled world today, will we ever find,
There is no child abuse, or cruelty of any kind?
Like our firm intentions, can these promises be kept?
Can these things ever be, when there's no respect?
We make new resolutions, when a new year does begin,
But only in a short time, they end up in the bin!

*Glenice Siddall*

## New Beginnings

Your bag,
New,
Pink,
Mesh,
Top tying,
Enclosing,
Amniotic fluid,
Hiding birth,
New beginnings,
A womb of
Emotions,
Waiting to be
Born;
Love, painful,
Jealous, torn,
Hope, feisty,
Determination, strong.
Unfathomable
Feelings,
Waiting to belong.
We tied the
Top of your
New pink
Bag,
Our eyes
Engaging,
Ecstatic,
Sad.
But our love is enduring
Will survive the surge.
No one knows
What emotions
Will emerge.

*Janet M Baird*

## ENLIGHTENED SCEPTICISM

The microbe is so very small
You cannot make him out at all.
But many clever people hope
To see him through a microscope.

A micro-organism's got
To stay so small so we cannot
Do more than just hypothesise
In blind and often wild surmise,
About his looks, his DNA,
And does he thrive on IPA?

His serried rows of tiny teeth,
His purple eyes that lie beneath
His tufted tails, insouciant,
That thrash the air, impatient.
His little legs aquamarine,
Have never, ever yet been seen . . .
But scientists, who ought to know,
Assure us that he must look so . . .
Oh, never, ever, let us doubt
What nobody's quite sure about!

In taking this example of suspended disbelief,
It's surely not irrational for us to seek relief
From critical appraisal, mental effort then eschewing,
Accepting that our leaders know precisely what they're doing.

From Downing Street, Westminster, and from Whitehall down to us,
It seems to me it makes most sense when viewed as pure chaos.
But, trust our leaders, who I'm sure know just what is ensuing;
They are experts, and we are not: they'll know just what they're doing!

*Patrick Brady*

# THE PERFECT TIME

They could introduce themselves;
sleep,

or try again.
Instead they just lie there

side by side
back to back

staring into space
thoughts as transparent

as their cigarette smoke drifting
on separate trails to the ceiling.

They should get up and dress
but they wait.

This would be
the perfect time . . .

***Les Merton***

# A PILGRIM'S WAY

Life is so precious as we journey on,
With the greatest friend as we walk along,
On Mother Earth we all do love so dear,
Thankful for the little while we have here.
To be a pilgrim, journey day by day,
In the steps of Jesus, who is the way.
He is our loving shepherd, we His sheep,
Made the one sacrifice, His fold to keep.
We follow by faith and with hearts of love,
Till our journey ends, with Heaven above!

*Joan Egre*

## 2004 - THE YEAR OF PEACE?

When Blair awoke on New Year's Day
He saw the graves where soldiers lay,
He wept and stood and stared in awe,
Then murmured sadly, 'No more war,'
In my dreams . . .

Sharon awoke on New Year's morn
To doom and death, to strife and scorn,
He cursed the blood, the blight, the bomb,
And whispered soft, 'Shalom, Shalom,'
In my dreams . . .

The faceless men on New Year's Eve
Told widowed women not to grieve,
But as the body bags returned
George W Bush, for peace he yearned,
In my dreams,
In my dreams,
In my dreams . . .

*Peter Davies*

## KING OF SPEED

He was moving so fast
I had to run to keep up.
I wondered if I could last -
The pace.
So I asked this ace a question.
How can you change from zero
To one and back?
And he fixed me with a steely gaze
That seemed to shimmer,
As though in a heat haze
Created by the blur
Of his being.
Then he smiled
And legends became real.
Suddenly I knew the answer -
It's not what you see,
It's what you feel.

He was the king of speed
And he taught me all he knew
About the mysteries of the universe
And the doors you must pass through
When you reach out
With your mind
And separate the old from the new.

*R G Whatley*

## POEM FOR ANDON

We believe this truth, you are living proof
That true love is life defining,
You express the brief of our joint belief
In a cloud-like silver lining.

In the ancient halls, down the canyon walls
Where the night falls soft as heather,
All our dreams evolve, as the stars revolve,
And the echoes last forever.

As the days speed by, like the eagles fly,
High above the earthen prison,
We will try to dry, every tear you cry,
So your love will be arisen.

With our stops and starts, with our aching hearts,
Watch you walk through streets of towers,
And the memory, parts of you and we
As the minutes turn to hours.

When we fall and bleed, you are all we need
To piece us back together;
We believe the truth, you're the living proof
That true love will be forever.
*'Poetic tributes'.*

**Tony Bush**

## ADOPTED

A cuckoo left in strange nest to
Grow and mend
For frantic new parents to
Love and tend
Till bursting point
Till harmony is lost into the wind.

Then into the wild free air
I fly
Painful moorings
Cast aside
Powerless to hold me now in this
My childlike reach for the sky.

***Anna Shannon***

## HAPPY NEW YEAR?

So you're going to give up smoking
Or lose that excess weight?
Good resolutions, as they stand
But I'm going to tell you straight

That I dread the new year coming.
I'm afraid of what's in store.
Are there any more disasters
To befall me? For I'm not sure

I wouldn't want another year
Like the one that has just gone;
A year when my darling daddy
And a best friend, both passed on.

When our health, not at its best
Caused anxiety and fear.
No, two thousand and three
Was not our best year.

So, I've made no resolutions,
No promises or plans.
I'll take each day as it comes
And do the best I can.

Yet I have my fingers crossed
That the new year will hold
Less of the sad times
And more joy, as yet untold.

*Olivia Collins*

# NEW YEAR THOUGHTS

The new year tiptoed lightly upon me
Softly, peacefully, extremely low-key
Warm kisses, and a glowing goodwill toast
Just being with those I love most
Calls, emails from near and far
Connecting, commuting by plane, boat and car
Reminiscing, remembering many, dreams of old
Anticipating new horizons, plans brave and bold
A time for new beginnings, a fresh start
Good wishes, encouragement straight from the heart
Reassuring words of advice for my musical son
Stay steadfast and strong on the path you've begun
Music flows through your veins like a river of love
A special gift bestowed on you, from above
Keep chasing your dreams; they will all come true
Fame is just around the corner waiting for you
Prayers, thoughts of absent friends and family gone away
Lovingly reunited in spirit this New Year's Day.

*Angela Moore*

# MY NEW TITLE

In 1960 at the birth of my son
I was what you call a real happy mum
As the years passed and my son grew
I was the proudest of mums that you ever knew.

He was in the RAF and that was his life
Then he met a young girl and made her his wife
She'd been married before but that was no crime
All in the family thought she was fine.

A step-daughter of three made my son glad
He was delighted when she called him 'Dad'
I was as helpful as all mums can be
And thought it was lovely when 'Nan' she called me

My step granddaughter now has a man in her life
A date has been fixed when she'll be his wife
When they have a family I hope they have the fun
That I always got from my first born son

I'll get out the needles and start knitting a coat
Then I can stand there and maybe gloat
I'll then have a title surpassing no other
That title will be your child's great grandmother!

*L Snow*

## PAST/BEGINNING/FRIENDS

My life was dark, just like the night,
with no shining stars that would have shone so bright.
For there was no hope, or leap of faith,
until one day I had a change of fate.
For that was my past, and you are my beginning,
for I'm so happy that my heart keeps on singing.
For you are the sun that shines in my heart,
keeping me warm until it gets dark.
For you are always in my thoughts and forever in my heart
and even though that we are sometimes distant,
we will never be far apart.
For you are my friend, that I care for so much
that it hurts me sometimes when you don't keep in touch.
I know that you are sometimes busy
and can't always make time for me,
but I will still carry you in my heart,
and be there for you whenever you need me.

*Clare L Pantling*

## A New Beginning

What better time for a new beginning
Than the beginning of the year.
A new era, new ideas, new friends, new interests.
What better time for a new beginning
Than the beginning of each day.
We can put behind us past mistakes, and words spoken in anger.
Every day is a new beginning.
From the break of day, all is fresh and clear.
We can vow to do better in our daily lives, to begin again the
task of living.

To see all ages start afresh each day.
The most beautiful beginning of all though
Is to see a new born babe.
That is the beginning of life.

*Janet Cavill*

## NEW BEGINNINGS

New thoughts, new dreams, away the past
old lessons learnt, a new net cast.

Bent walking lives, now upright, strong,
no wasted years in life's long song.

Fresh smiles of warmth to dent the din
let's tears laugh and crying sing.

New lightened life for those less certain
an empty stage, a new raised curtain.

The long goodbye to years well done
old lessons learnt, a new day dawns.

The calling light from bolted dark
it leaves a smile and dreams unmarked

Look to the warm out from the dusk
let shadows still and leave no mask.

New fresh scents and pastures green
await to free what could have been.

See beauty free in all life's burdens
it's waiting there, I know it's certain.

The past's washed fresh, a well-trodden mile
the time is ripe for life's long smile.

So glow and glow, and grin and sing
taste lightness sweet, and want and win.

Grasp fresh anew the present taste
the future's now, the past a waste.

Let nature's beauty remove the grind
the past's well spent, the future blind.

*Nigel Sinkins*

## ANOTHER TALE TO TELL

It closed, that book. With all the pages
Tattered and torn. A hundred times read,
Devoured, even
With the hunger and delicate ferocity of
The new born babe.
An epic. A fanciful adventure that
Dreams are made of.

The writer and the reader sat back.
Watching through clouded lenses
At the tale as though it never were.
And then another. Another tale
With no end, no middle.
Barely even a beginning.
And they begin, etching out the path
And twists and turns,
Each rain drops and flower blooms,
And the tale
Unfolds.

*Rhian Watkins*

## CROSSROADS

I stand at the crossroads
What shall I do?
Back there is safety,
Forward, there's you.

You, with your laughter
And come to bed eyes,
Your after dark kisses
And warm loving sighs.

Behind me, security
And dead, dull routine,
A life of regret
Wondering what might have been.

I stand at the crossroads,
Suitcase in hand,
Uncertain, unsure,
Of the life that we've planned.

What if the promises
Turn out to be lies,
From the man with warm kisses
And come to bed eyes.

Perhaps on the other side
The grass won't be green,
There's much to be said
For dead, dull routine.

I stand at the crossroads,
Here comes the bus,
I'm climbing aboard
To the future, and us.

*Joyce Walker*

# A NEW TOWN CENTRE

Strollers talking
traders dealing
shoppers walking
push-chairs wheeling

leave the arcade for the square
pause to see what's happening there

perched over heads only the chunky clock's hands clap noon

magazine vendors
youthful spenders
a guitar player
a firebrand juggler

laughter and jostlings all interweave
whilst students sing 'I ain't gonna grieve'

a loose fluttering tissue amazes the pigeons

high heels wobbling
beat a ticking click
sets lads' heads turning
for their whistling trick

tabloid readers stretch on benches
couples lounge two in clinches

a flower stall's bright bunches add perfume to beauty

old benchers chatting
racing children skip
some smokers wafting
groups of gigglers gossip

town folks are laughing the bright day away
as the square is vibrant in the middle of the day.

*Dennis Marshall*

## SENTINELS

*(Abridged)*

One hundred, two hundred, three hundred strong,
Standing on guard, just where we belong,
Watching silently, across the long barrow,
Just where the roads become very narrow.

Long, long ago, our ancestors stood watch,
Just as we do now, on this sacred patch,
Bronze age people, their dead were interred,
On top of the ridgeway, just where they preferred.

My ancestors went the way of all living,
They died and decayed, after years of their giving.
Guard to those now milleniums gone,
Away in the dark of the setting sun.

Slowly, we grew to take their place,
And carried on watching the human race.
Re-discovering the bronze age days,
When across the ridgeway, your people gazed.

Digs went on, and deep they found,
Chariots of chiefs buried deep underground.
Respect to your past is very much due,
What is your future? You haven't a clue!

Look at us here, sentinels standing,
Watching as humankind is expanding,
Filling the planet, it's really not good
To chop us all down, because you need wood.

My brothers, my sisters, here we all lie,
Doomed by your woodman now to die,
Our bodies lie so tall, yet so narrow,
Just in the shade of the bronze age barrow.

Beauteous we were and useful as well,
What happens next we really can't tell,
As I lie dying beside the barrow
That stands by the road that is long and narrow.

*Mary Joan Boyd*

# I AM BLESSED

I am rich in the things that really matter in life,
my health, and happiness, wonderful friends,
I am so very blessed with an abundance,
that seems to have no end.
A life filled with peace and love,
family reaching far and wide,
real friends and my children,
my loving husband by my side.
Music for my ears to hear,
a bed in which to sleep,
food for my belly,
and a roof that doesn't leak.
A bounty from the garden,
sacred time for myself,
there really is no way,
to measure the profusion of this wealth.
Hands that can reach out,
and a heart that can heal
beholden to this blessing,
my life . . . so very real.
*I am blessed*

**Kitty Morgan**

## COUNTDOWN TO HAPPINESS

Ten, nine, eight, seven, six, five, four, three, two and one,
Big Ben is striking midnight, the old year now is done.

The new year is upon us but please don't you feel blue,
It is time to send the old away and welcome in the new.

New year and new beginnings, I wonder what they'll be,
Well, only time will tell that, you will have to wait and see.

I hope it brings you happiness, who or wherever you may be,
So have a happy new year, with love to you from me.

*Kram*

## New Year Resolutions

As the old year departs into history
What our future will hold is a mystery
Unwritten, unmapped, it's for us to tread
Go with hope in your heart and not with dread.

The past is gone and all finished now
Only the future ahead, so make a vow
To learn from the past, then let it go
Look forward not back, it is best you know.

Remember the good times and savour each one
Find comfort from knowing the bad ones are gone
Walk on with courage to face the new day
Your life awaits you to live it your way.

Search for your dreams, seek every one out
You deserve to be happy so have no doubt
Believe in yourself and the year ahead
Go with hope in your heart and not with dread.

*Patricia Susan Dixon MacArthur*

## IN THE THOUGHTS BEFORE DREAMS

I saw her standing all alone,
The grass above her knees
Her finger tips caressed the tops
Of blades moved by the breeze.

I saw her pains and worries slip,
As sunshine warmed her through.
And rubbed her back, eased her soul,
Beneath the bluest blue.

Her only child danced in the blades,
That came up to his waist.
And both now danced in different ways,
As time now lost its haste.

The big oak tree, just to her left,
Was tall and strong and proud.
It also danced beneath the blue,
That bore no single cloud.

I watched and then I saw a man
Move close and take her hand.
And as I saw them kiss I knew,
She was complete as planned.

***Sid 'de' Knees***

## LIFE CYCLE

They begin as minute inky specks,
Encased in a spherical gelatinous chamber,
Suspended as hundreds of trapped apostrophes.
Transformed, they emerge as free swimming
Aquatic creatures with a tail.

In a season they metamorphose,
Issuing from ditches and pools in droves,
Forsaking, for a time, their watery existence,
Searching for cool, damp places to hibernate.

As the warmer days of spring return,
Small, perfectly-formed amphibians
Revisit the waters of their birth.
Among masses of heaving, bulging bodies,
Males croak boisterously, in arduous attempts
To grasp a mate, endeavouring to secure
The survival of their species.

*Liam Heaney*

## SPRING WILL COME

All the leaves are turning brown,
They're all falling from the trees
And lying on the ground.
And the birds, they make no sound,
They just stand there on the grass,
Their heads bowed; they have no song.

And spring will come, as you promised,
But not yet.
My grieving's still not done.
Far as I'm concerned, time can stand still,
So I can repeat, you're still the only one.

Yes, I know it's been months now
And my friends are telling me
I really should go out.
Yes, I promised to move on
And we talked of how I'd be
Once you'd gone. I'd carry on.
I promised to remember that spring will come.
Spring will come.

*John Coughlan*

# DIARY

On a shelf collecting dust
There lay a diary, just forgotten.
The cover with its ragged edging,
The embroidery upon some cotton.

I blew the dust off from the cover,
I flicked the blank lined pages,
I sniffed the diary with all my might,
Ideas then escaped from cages.

My boredom (which is pain to me)
Will hopefully just disappear,
For in this diary I will keep
My thoughts, my hopes and all I fear.

I shall write inside my diary daily!
And I shall keep my diary neat!
I'll write and I promise not to fail!
And then my boredom I'll defeat!

*Elena Uteva*

## WORLD OF?

World of anger, world of pain,
World of sadness, world of rain,
World of wonder, world of awe,
What kind of world will *you* make in 2004?

World of torture, world of jeer,
World of danger, world of fear,
World of freedom, world of fun,
World of summer, world of sun.

World of winter, world of ice,
World of horror, world of vice,
World of wonder, world of awe,
What kind of world will *we* make in 2004?

***Lorraine Green***

## CHERISHED THOUGHTS

The year had so much promise for me
A new life begun so pure and sweet
Time to sit back, listen and retreat
A grandchild's love and a mother's smile
All gifts to keep from God above

A dream come true with a child's success
So many moments to cherish and express
My mind ticked on so much inside
To plan and hope for the world I cried.
The new beginning for terrorism to go
Crime to strike down to an all-time low
But the new beginning would have it all
So much to see in a global overhaul.
The trend for greed and commercial boom
No more talk of doom and gloom.

A new beginning to work things out
Nations together to love not shout.

*Karen Smith*

# New Beginnings

As I embark on a new journey
Of waters not known before,
I look forward to making
My dreams come true.

I paint with visual impairments
Knowing God makes it possible,
With extra help through lighting
And other aids to help me.

I look forward to woodcarving using
An electric carving tool,
Giving me the scope to shape
And carve birds and animals,
In ways not thought possible
As I learn to live with a disability.

I look forward to a new start
With lots of opportunities
That are now open for me,
As God opens new doors.

*Julie Smith*

## MY NEW LIFE

There are three of us here, but I'm alone in this pool,
Olympic-sized, with shiny aqua walls,
Cool ripples dowsing my face.
A refreshing breeze blows through the tall window
And someone is soaking in the frothy spa foam,
Unaware of my presence.

I manage a length a minute in sure, measured moves,
Whilst serious swimmers skim past in swift, sleek waves of sound,
Goggles on, bobbing in butterfly bounds
Or slicing through the silver water with shark-like back fins.

And then it's over: I'm out, I'm dried, I'm dressed, I'm done.
(For today at least).

It's been four months now in my prison cell, but seems a life sentence:
I miss the bustle and the colour of cheerful, busy lives,
The buzz of chatter and the witty repartee.

My solitary confinement suffocates,
The vicious stranglehold of illness choking me,
Prodding me awake hourly in startling stabs of fear,
Drenched bedsheets in a tormenting tide,
Condemned to icy shivers,
Barefoot on the landing.

As the nausea attacks launch their vice-like grip,
The numbness of insomnia resumes its vigil.

And then the tiny miracle:

With one night's sleep I see
A pin-prick of light at the end of
This long, black tunnel of
Stress.

Like the moth emerging from the chrysalis,
Unsteady on sticky wings,
My flight path appears.

*Kay Jude*

## MY NEW YEAR RESOLUTIONS

There's no point putting moisture back into the ends
when the real problem is much nearer your roots.
I usually have pale skin and dark circles under my eyes
but in summer, when I get a tan, people tell me how well I look.
Next, pick up a little powder on a big brush and lightly dust over cheeks,
nose, forehead and chin.
Do you blast it with a dryer or load it with styling products?
This heat the wall of the blood vessel, causing it to break down
completely . . . what do I look like?
You'll feel a sharp sting, but the short treatment time makes it easy
to bear . . . did I think well?
I was 24 weeks pregnant and I'd just gone to bed when my waters broke
. . . where was my world?
I had to face up to it, tears in my eyes, why?
I called out to my husband - he came running into the bedroom.
'It's not time yet,' he said.
'Cross your legs or something.'
*Oh men, oh men,* I thought.
A born fighter ... born fighter - I'm on this day.
For three years I evaded the inevitable...in all my thoughts.
It's been a terrible time, but I'm glad we talked about everything
before it was too late.
The paramedics arrived almost immediately and took me to the
big general hospital.
I was wheeled to the nearest maternity ward and within an hour . . .
Elle-Mai was born.
She weighed 11lb 6oz and wasn't breathing . . . more tears again.
I said, 'She's not going to make it,' so sad I am right now.
I didn't want to take a moment away . . . or talk about it.
Despite that Elle-Mai put up a strong fight, hour after hour.
She had heart surgery and it was successful . . . many months
to wait for good or bad news.

Even when she had to return to the ventilator, she displayed her spirit and gradually gained more strength.

Eventually I was able to take her home . . . after 6 long months.

Now Elle-Mai is 10 months old and she's improving all the time.

It was bizarre and the best day of my life . . . to hold her in my arms for the first time.

You are my heroine, you only had 25% chance of survival.

It was everything I'd hoped for . . . she is so beautiful.

I knew I'd married the right man, because he made me feel very special every day.

'Well done,' he said. Our little daughter . . . she's a real beauty.

***Viv Lionel Borer***

# OLD LOVE RENEWED

Enmeshed in a net, concealed in a trap
Holding on tightly for how long it lasts
Caught in a world not known before
A mystic world, and still seeking more.

Enveloped in darkness, yet stars burning bright
Inky black tendrils that hold me this night
Unfolding secrets, long since held hidden
Of a time when my passion, kept total forbidden.

Don't know how to react, if advantages were
To be released to move freely, would that I dare
Like being caught in a maelstrom, such a dilemma
My thoughts intermingle, *Can this be forever?*

Now thinking more clearly, no end in sight
Enjoying the moment of this endless twilight
Still trying to analyse what could be in store
If this were love, could I ask for more?

My memory recalls sweet dreams of the past
When I was confronted, and my life put to task
We both made decisions we thought for the best
*Is it right to start over?* with so little time left.

*J Prentice*

## OPEN SCHEDULE

Tomorrow I'll begin.
It's not here, yet not far away.
Distant enough to be comfortable.
I still have today, to sort
myself out,
wrestle with doubt.
Yes, tomorrow is perfect.
Today is a reject.
Tomorrow will be
the first day
of the rest
of my
life.

*Dawn Sansum*

## THE SEASONS' PARADE

In the distance, the sound of the cannon's fire blasts,
As a parade of the seasons once more goes past.
It's the start of yet another new year,
Goodbye to the old, let's shed a small tear.

A performance of seasons is about to begin,
The doors have just opened; winter's already in.
Dressed in cold darkness, yet warmth lies inside,
Tempting all souls for to sleep far and wide.

A fanfare of colours, church bells will ring,
Bravo! as enters magnificent spring.
With her cascade of flowers, a month of new birth,
The magic of nature ascends from the earth.

Summer will follow, the season at best,
Splendour around us, it's full of pure zest.
Flowers are blooming, trees in full flow,
Sunshine has helped all these wonders to grow.

As summer steps out with her usual grace,
We see autumn arrive with her beautiful face.
Mature with such wisdom, she puts things away,
Preparing all things for returning one day.

Once autumn has passed and tidied away,
It's now time for winter to come out and play.
How brilliant to have a parade for to view,
Just leave it to nature, she knows what to do.

*Betty Hattersley*

## REACH OUT AND TOUCH ME

O Lord, I'm needy, weak, dried out
Without an anchor sure.
I'm tossed about in turmoil and
I've troubles by the score.

I thought that I'd get through this mess
By burying my head.
Pretending everything was fine,
Trusting myself instead.

But as I paused a gentle voice
Was heard so clear and plain.
'My child reach out and touch me now
And you'll be whole again.

I'm here to minister and heal,
To guide you, bring you through
To higher ground which I've prepared.
My child, you'll be brand new!'

***Gillian Humphries***

# LIBERATING THE GHOST IN THE COWL

I see the figure shrouded by a cowl.
He stands almost hidden in the shadows.
Hurt and lonely, he sees no one.
He has stood thus, since crossing over.
His life ending in such a trauma,
In some terrible, explosive event.
His body is barely recognisable.
Now his earthbound ghost remains unclaimed.
He knows not that his soul remains unblemished.
Too many earthbound spirits remain here,
Yet he is caught in a void of his own.
A bitter realm; empty, silent and cold.
Now I am instructed to go to him.
Plead with this suffering entity.
I am bid to free his blighted soul.
I reveal myself to this poor being.
Overwhelmed by his endless suffering,
Shocked in fact by what he looked like
On this unfortunate one's demise.
But guided and supervised
By the old ones of the living light,
My metaphysical arms
In compassion embrace him.
I am driven to kiss his ravaged face.
This is truly loving thing.
The healing for him now begins.
A cessation of his suffering,
Like a snake sheds its aged skin.
A soul renewed in perfection,
Swallowed by the descending light.

*Jonathan Pegg*

# VICTORIOUS NOT VICTIM

Precious layers stripped away,
Raw and naked core exposed.
Shutting down all future hope,
My eyes and mind are closed.

But the bitter winter wind awakes,
Shakes, makes my fibres tough,
I rise triumphant, not defeated,
Screaming, 'I have had enough!'

*Kerri Fordham*

# A New Leaf

There's a new leaf upon the tree
A thousand, thousand have been before
In the life of this great tree
Yet, the tree rejoices, and is glad
For there is a new leaf upon the tree

The roots are deep and hidden
'Tis one tree from root to branch
And lives in and through each leaf
The heart's smile resurrected
Through the new leaf upon the tree

Like the stars of Heaven
New leaves have been many
And so they all are one
For they all share the same root
Bless the new leaf upon the tree

Perfection in the blessing
Joy released in tears of love
The strength in life will comfort
From root to God above
A new leaf upon the tree

Beauty, truth and life
Complete from root to branch
When life's cycle turns
Leaves fall to nourish roots
And behold, a new leaf upon the tree

*A R Wait*

## New Beginning

A new beginning is
a newly-wed couple
sharing love and happiness.

A new beginning is
a new home
bringing security and warmth.

A new beginning is
a new born baby
bringing joy and pleasure.

*Catrina Lawrence*

## NEW BEGINNINGS

Opening a new book,
meeting new people,
learning a new hobby,
weaving a new life,
all undertaken with a child's enthusiasm
or the exuberance of nature around us.
Like a new-born baby
innocent and so alive,
we touch these moments with joy.
The mystery of new life enthrals
in its beauty and simplicity.

*Margaret Ann Wheatley*

## Do I Have To Make A Resolution?

Another new year,
time to make a resolution.
Perhaps I could stop
world pollution!

No, I can't do that.
Was only joking.
But I could begin
by giving up smoking.

There must be something
I should do.
Can anyone help me,
give me a clue?

Yes! Lose some weight.
It's a good idea.
I'll give it more thought
(later in the year).

I could get a job
and earn big money.
Have holidays abroad,
somewhere nice and sunny.

It's such hard work,
and time-consuming,
making resolutions,
and February's looming.

And what's the point
of all this, really?
When I'm obviously perfect,
well . . . almost . . . nearly!

*Gillian L Bestwick*

# A RESOLUTION
*(For those that know they matter)*

So what shall I do this New Year
That's so different from the last?
What can just one man possibly do
To make up for the whole world's past?

Where does one start to make amends
For the wrongs we've done each other?
Each commandment sadly cast aside,
Crimes committed against one another.

Perhaps I should start with those closest to me
Let them know what they really mean:
Their strength and support has been solid
And my true gratitude needs to be seen.

You all know just what I want the most
As this sorrowful year reaches its end.
But apart from this, I feel honoured
Because I have you all, as my friends.

So this year I will try to be worthy
Of the faith that you all hold in me.
But a father, a son, a brother, a friend,
I promise, forever to be:

***John Osland***

# INFORMATION

We hope you have enjoyed reading this book - and that you will continue to enjoy it in the coming years.

If you like reading and writing poetry drop us a line, or give us a call, and we'll send you a free information pack.

Alternatively if you would like to order further copies of this book or any of our other titles, then please give us a call or log onto our website at www.forwardpress.co.uk

**Anchor Books Information
Remus House
Coltsfoot Drive
Peterborough
PE2 9JX
(01733) 898102**